The Links of Life

The Links of Life

DAN CHUKE

Story Terrace

Text Dan Chuke

Design StoryTerrace

Copyright © Dan Chuke

Text is private and confidential

First print July 2022

StoryTerrace

www.StoryTerrace.com

CONTENTS

Dear Dad,

The ones who love you want to hear your story, and my God, what a story! I'm glad that you agreed it is a story worth telling.

You have blessed us by always being a felt presence in our lives.

You bless us even more by letting us know you better in this way.

I hope you enjoyed recollecting and recounting your story as much as I have enjoyed feasting on your every word.

Thank you for your love and support and especially for simply being dad.

Happy 80th birthday!
Love,
Chiamaka

1

THE LINKS OF LIFE

Nowadays you will often find me on a golf course, where I can get bad breaks from good shots and good breaks from bad shots, but I have to play the ball from where it lies. My life has been like that; I have made the most of every opportunity in which I have found myself. During a game of golf, it's the follow-through that makes the difference, and I have always seen through the choices I have made. My daughter, Chiamaka, has asked me to share my story with you, so let me begin to tell you where the fairways of life have led me!

I was born in Enugu on 11th September 1942, the youngest of the six children of John Aniegboka Chuke, an employee of the Nigerian Railways Corporation, then known as Government Department of Railways, and his wife Anna Chibunma, both of whom hailed from Obosi. Sadly, my second eldest brother, Hyacinth died in infancy, and my father had died on Sunday May 24, 1942 just four months before I was born. While my two sisters and my eldest brother went to live with our uncle in Ajali, where he was a schoolteacher, my mother raised me and my immediate elder brother in Obosi, Anambra State, Eastern Nigeria, instilling in us the morals and work ethic that were to carry me through life with success and happiness. My mother was always looking out to help others and she brought me up to have a positive attitude. Just as golf is about how well you accept and respond to your misses rather than achieving a perfect score, I have been able to adapt to any challenge.

I had a happy childhood, and I was fortunate to have several strong role models, including my eldest brother, Paul; I strove to follow in his footsteps in several areas of life.

Faith has become the rock of my life, and I have never let myself become so absorbed in the whirlwind of work as to forget about God. My grandfather, Igwe Chuke, had a very strong faith and encouraged the Catholic missionaries headquartered in Onitsha to spread their missionary activities to our town of Obosi. He felt impelled to provide temporary accommodation for a place of worship plus a school. His siblings Onuekwusi and Obieze later agreed to donate a large piece of family land for the erection of a permanent school and church.

I attended this school, which was called St Theresa's Catholic School, and all the descendants of my great-grandfather, Eze Otagwo, were supposed to receive free education there. Unfortunately, this did not always happen, but things were rectified, and in compensation the school's name was changed to Chuke Memorial School.

When we were growing up, our village, like most others, did not have electricity or running water. Those were luxuries enjoyed only in the cities. River Idemili provided the water we needed for our chores (cooking and washing). It was an arduous task to carry the water clay pot or galvanised steel bucket on our heads up from the steep valley along the sandy path. Our shoeless feet would feel the scorching heat of the ground.

We all believed that the river was the home of Idemili, the deity that protected our town. We would always go in groups to collect water, and the first group that arrived early in the morning had to chant an incantation to ensure that the deity continued to dwell peacefully within the river, and then we would enter, fill our container and bathe before going home and then to school.

In the river we learned by practice how to swim; this was an advantage over city children, who did not have this opportunity. Sadly, we had occasions when over exuberant or not properly initiated children ventured in too deeply and lost their lives. We all accepted and respected the fact that the fish in the river belonged to Idemili, so we would not catch and eat them. If we discovered any in our water buckets, we always found a way to keep them alive before we returned them to the river so as not to incur the wrath of the deity or to fall foul of a curse. It was always fun to go to the stream to fetch water, especially after school, for it provided an extra opportunity to play with other children, in addition to the joy of watching monkeys jumping and playing on the several trees lining both sides of the river. The river also offered a practice ground for somersaulting, an art which has become the trademark of Obosi youths in sports and entertainment. Historically, Obosi people honoured the royal python, which is dedicated to Idemili. Killing this species of python is considered a great sacrilege, and if one is killed, it should be buried with the full funeral rites normally reserved for a human being.

Mother cooked yams, cassava and beans, with a variety of vegetables. Rice wasn't grown in our area, so any rice dish was a rare treat. I often helped Mother by going to the farm for the yams or cassava after school, or I would venture into the forest to collect firewood. In the farmlands close to where the River Idemili met the River Niger, an occasional rhino could be sighted. Rumours spread of how a farmer had to spend the night on a tree because a parading rhino refused to leave the area. A famous hunter in the town, Ben Iwenofu, was said to have shot and killed a lion in the forest around the farmlands. A photograph of the hunter and the dead lion hung on a wall in his house.

We lived in a raised bungalow on a foundation of compressed red laterite; the house is still standing today, 85 years after it was built, and the thick gauge corrugated steel roof has never leaked. How many times have I flown up those six flights of steps, ravenous after school, to be met by my mother and some of her delightful cooking? The walls were constructed of red mud unfired bricks, plastered with cement. The porch of the bungalow had six wooden windows; each window had four vertical steel rods for security reasons. I was an active child, and I would climb up to the windowsill and try to sneak headfirst through the gap between two of the vertical bars. One day when I had grown older – I had also grown bigger of course – and I know you will guess what is coming next! Yes, I got my head well and truly stuck between the rods. I was scared stiff, as was my mother; it was also quite sad because that was the end of one of my schoolboy pranks!

The best thing about our bungalow was that the house was built by my father and his younger brother, James, to house their families, so it truly was a house built on fraternal love, and it was special to grow up knowing that my father, whom I had never met, had built this house for my siblings and me. A long corridor meant that it felt like two separate homes.

On the links, success depends less on strength of body and more on strength of mind and character. My mother and my siblings showed me that anything is possible when you have the right people to support you; they helped me to develop the mental and spiritual approach to life that led me, a small village boy, to rise through the ranks to become CEO of a government investment company.

My mother, Ogbueshi Nwanyi Anna Chibumma Chuke

My mum and dad in 1930

Dan Chuke-Affaa Obosi

With His Grace, Most Rev. Dr. Valerian Okeke, The Metropolitan Archbishop Onitsha Province of the Catholic Church

2

AIMING FOR PAR

Obosi provided us with a stable start in life. At that time, it was a small, caring society; we would never have believed that it would grow to be the densely populated city it is today. The founder of Obosi was a hunter named Adike, from Ojoto, and the name Obosi came from 'mbosisi', meaning 'falling apart of soil'. Adike called the village this because of the difficulties he encountered building his house due to the easily eroded soil.

Everyone helped each other out in our close-knit community. My immediate elder brother, Boniface, affectionately known as Bon, lived with my mother and me in the bungalow. I have mentioned that my father had passed away, but he had only been in his early 40s, so my mother would naturally have struggled financially without her breadwinner. Until my two older sisters, Beatrice and Agatha started work as schoolteachers after their training and took over the care of our needs including secondary school fees for Bon and me, my mother's brother Linus

Okafor was our benevolent supporter. He would send my mother dried fish from the north to sell in order to augment her income from farming and dress making.

In the game of golf, I know from experience that every shot counts. Through my education at St Theresa's Catholic Primary School in Obosi and Secondary School at Christ the King College Onitsha, I was aware of the butterfly effect. If my grandfather had not been proactive in trekking to Onitsha with his cousin Anazonwu to persuade the missionaries to establish in Obosi and offering them temporary accommodation for church and school in his compound, life for many would have been very different. I was always aware that the Irish priests had established their mission here due to my grandfather, and therefore, I respected my inheritance of determination, foresight and an altruistic approach. I understood from an early age that every step I took would shape my future.

The Anglican missionaries came into Obosi before the Catholics but, with healthy competition and cooperation, they succeeded in turning Obosi into a town where education and high moral values became most sought after. They encouraged the abolition of the Osu and Oru caste system and introduced modern healthcare, providing treatment for leprosy.

I have few memories of life at my primary school, but they are all happy. Francis Molokwu Stephen Anyalogbu and Stephen Mgbakogu were my special friends, and I am saddened that they are no longer alive. Yet they will always live on in my memories of our soccer games, which were the love of our schooldays. We would play whenever we could, and if we couldn't get our hands on a football outside school, we'd even substitute home-made raw rubber wrapped around anything spherical! In school we had football teams that played in hotly contested competition against other teams from different schools in the local government area. I was also in the church choir, which sometimes stole me away from my beloved game. I continued to dream of becoming a soccer star, but in those days being a footballer was not considered a great career because players were not paid the huge salaries they receive now.

I recall the happiness of Christmas Day as a child, the excitement of midnight mass on Christmas Eve, maybe morning mass and then the delight of lunch of rice with chicken or maybe fish. My friends and I would visit homes, like some children do at Halloween in America and Europe, to collect gifts of money, biscuits and sweets from neighbouring friends. Masquerades performed all over the town and everyone would stop and watch the different shows. Females would watch from safe distances as only males could be initiated into the masquerade cult. Religious rites of passage such as baptisms, confirmations or first communions meant everything to us. Baptism was mostly done in infancy, but First Communion and confirmation were really special – the conclusion of many preparation classes. Obosi Catholic Mission was then part of the parish of Umuoji, a town about five kilometres to the east. That was where we had to trek for these great events which meant that we had to wake up early and perform our normal morning chores before the journey.

The route to Umuoji was lined with mango trees and passion week, first communion and confirmation were usually done during the Easter period which coincides with ripening of mangoes. The joy of receiving the sacrament and the adventure of climbing mango trees to harvest the delicious fruits made the occasion unforgettable. I still recall the immaculate white trousers and shirt, the feeling of triumph for attaining that level of achievement and recognition in the church and how the dresses were marred with sweat, dust and yellowish mango stains by the time we got home.

In addition to the Christian festivities, we also celebrated our traditional festivals. Most families had farmlands of their own which they farmed to provide food throughout the year. Yam was cultivated mainly by men but cassava, beans and vegetables mainly by the women and so, you can imagine that most festivals revolved around yam, the king of all crops. There were festivals to mark the beginning of the planting season and others to mark the harvest season. In fact, the first time the new yam is eaten, it is celebrated with pomp and pageantry by the Igwe (King), after which other households can then eat the new yam.

This festival called Obiora or Iwa Ji (cutting of yam) is still celebrated today and has become a yearly event when the Igwe dressed in resplendent traditional regalia displays his majesty to the admiration of his town folks and invited dignitaries with special music and traditional dances performed by various groups starting with the red capped chiefs. Various types of masquerades feature to add colour to the occasion. The subjects then pay homage to the Igwe by bringing presents. The Igwe uses the opportunity to honour deserving citizens and non-indigenes with various awards. The first king of Obosi was Eze Shime and the royal dynasty's genealogical tree dates back to 400 AD. Eze Shime bequeathed to his first two sons, Okwasala and Agu the right to rule the town. He was succeeded by Eze Agu. I descend from Eze Obodo, the first son of Eze Agu.

At the village school, I liked all my school subjects, but I especially excelled in arithmetic, English language, history, geography and religious studies – I would never have believed that one day I would visit so many of the countries we studied. I liked all the teachers, but it was a strict atmosphere, and if you were late to school, you would be caned. As our house was close to school because it had been built on our family land, you might think I would never have been late, but you would be wrong! Remember, I had chores to complete each morning before school, and if I was late out of bed, I had to race to fetch water or dash to the farm to collect provisions. I had the compound to sweep, the chickens to feed. Fetching firewood was usually an afternoon affair when you could clearly see and avoid snakes and other dangerous reptiles.

I was never really naughty at school because, as I have explained, I had been drilled in the honour of what my grandfather had achieved for us all. However, out of mischief, I sometimes hid others' books and pencils, for a laugh. As this was a mission school, religion was an important aspect of our education. The fear of hell was driven into the children, so that was another reason why I tried hard to do nothing really naughty. There weren't many cars on the roads in those days, so sometimes my friends and I played a game where we tried to hit passing cars with small sticks. If the drivers stopped, we always denied it was us, but afterwards when the drivers' serious words had faded from our ears, we felt very guilty!

Everyone strove to do well at school to please their parents, and I was always in the top ten in my class. I was on course for a successful future. My mother was over the moon when I passed the entrance exam to the prestigious secondary school Christ the King College (CKC) in Onitsha. I had done myself proud and brought honour to my grandfather's name. Everyone told me how proud my father would have been of me.

Life is so different today, but at the time we had no family holidays for sightseeing or leisure, apart from the occasional visit to a relative in another town for holidays. I remember with glee the time we went to stay with Mother's brother in Kano for the first time; I had travelled in a train, and it had taken more than a day to get there.

My new school was a boarding school, and although it was exciting to leave home to live with so many boys my own age, it was not without heartbreak. I loved my village, and I was very close to my mother, so it was inevitable that I would struggle with pangs of homesickness. However, as I looked down at the next fairway of life, I knew I would only get the chance to play one round, and I had to make the most of this fortunate opportunity. My goal was to achieve the West African school leavers' certificate after five years with flying colours, followed by the high school certificate with distinction, to allow me to proceed to a good university.

To overcome homesickness and also because of my love for sports, I kept myself occupied with table tennis, long tennis and, of course, soccer. I discovered that I had natural leadership qualities when I became the school captain for both lawn and table tennis. I was so proud when I was chosen to represent the school in soccer too.

I was appointed a school prefect by our Irish principal, and I knew such a position would be good for my future curriculum vitae and would further develop my qualities of responsibility, trustworthiness and respect for others. The roles I took on taught me to be cooperative and to develop a voice of authority, confidence and initiative. I learnt problem-solving skills and how to work as part of a group.

I had to go to the market in my role as food prefect to buy food for the school. This was rather a big responsibility for a young boy as I was trusted with money and a budget. The Irish fathers were very strict, and I had to account for every last penny of the money I was entrusted with; otherwise I would have received a severe scolding. However, we purchased rice in bulk from a wholesale contractor.

One day, our unsavoury rice supply contractor called me out of prep and offered me an envelope packed with money, which he termed a gesture of gratitude for winning the contract. He assured me that all the past food prefects had accepted this payment, but I refused to accept his dubious gift, for obvious reasons. I also said I was well provided for by my siblings, and I did not need this criminal money. There was no way I was going to destroy the skills and qualities that my positions of responsibility had afforded me; nor was I going to bring dishonour to the names of my grandfather and father. Success on the golf course depends on how effectively one learns to manage the two adversaries of the game: the course and oneself. I knew I had a chance to win at life if I stayed on par.

It was November when we noticed the rice supply was depleting faster than it should. The bags were not full. I informed the principal about the proposition that had been made to me, and the contract of the rice seller was immediately cancelled. The supplier had tried to bribe me to keep me quiet and not implicate him, but I wanted no place in such wrongdoing – it was against all the principles with which I had been raised.

During my time at boarding school, I did not go home each weekend, but once a month we got a free day on a Saturday when we could go out, but we had to return by six in the evening. If we couldn't travel home, we would explore the magnificent Onitsha market or participate in even more sporting fixtures. Every three months I always somehow found a way to return home for a holiday with Mum, whom I missed greatly. On my return I always helped my mother in the house or did odd jobs to offer her financial support.

Maths, additional maths, physics and chemistry plus Latin became my favourite subjects, and this led me to consider that I might enjoy a career in engineering. I joined the debating society, which further developed my talent for public speaking and communication skills. I learnt to be a critical and creative thinker.

I was a person who was more interested in outdoor pursuits than being indoors, and I also played hockey alongside any other outdoor sporting opportunities that passed my way. I showed no interest in boxing whatsoever; I abhorred violence in all its forms.

At our boarding school, a 'wash man' was employed who laundered our clothes, but we washed our underwear ourselves. The open dormitories each housed 60 students. Each dormitory had a prefect who had to keep the boys in order to ensure the dormitory and the environs were clean and tidy, that the students made their beds and observed silence once lights were out. Only the principal could whip the students, but the prefects could hand out lines to be done or order an erring student to go and mow the grass. I received that punishment a few times, but I tried not to retaliate when I was at the giving end!

Bullying of juniors as was prevalent in other schools around us was not tolerated in CKC. The principal was very particular in protecting the younger ones who he kept reminding us could become your senior in life. He would severely punish any senior students found to be harassing junior students, although the seniors sometimes frightened the juniors just by being bossy, and all juniors knew to keep out of the way of the prefects. True to the motto of the school, Bonitas Disciplina Scientia, good discipline was pre-eminent as a building block in the moulding of young minds and as far as the principal was concerned even the seniors must conduct themselves appropriately; they must dispense kindness to all and sundry.

The principal Rev. Fr. John Fitzpatrick was the ninth in line of the reverend Catholic priests who spearheaded in CKC the accomplishment of one of the primary objectives of the Catholic mission in Nigeria - evangelisation through education. He was popular among members of staff and students and was highly respected by his peers in other high-profile secondary schools in Nigeria. I can still picture him smoking his pipe; he was huge, a fair man with a commanding presence who only punished when necessary and hoped to instill good behaviour in more positive ways. He would gather Class V students in his office to listen to BBC news in an attempt to improve their spoken English. He was very proud and passionate about the school and wanted CKC to excel in every field of endeavour.

Fr. Fitzpatrick was transferred to develop a new school in 1963, my last year in CKC, and was replaced by the first indigenous principal - Rev. Fr. Nicholas Tagbo. The appointment of Fr. Nicholas was greeted with a loud ovation in the Christian community and it showed that the missionaries were succeeding in their objective, to evangelise and train the future trainers so that no vacuum is left when they eventually return home. As an alumnus, a member of the class of 1949 of CKC, he came with a mission. He not only maintained the passion of his predecessor to be a good disciplinarian and succeed in academics and sports, but he used his strong connection with the Old Boys Association to mobilise private funding and accomplish impressive structural developments within the school premises to provide more accommodation and recreational facilities.

The boys loved him so much that when he died in 2016 at the age of 87 years, the Old Boys Association organised a burial ceremony fit for kings. His gold trimmed casket mounted on a beautifully decorated carriage drawn by equally decorated horses paraded the streets of Onitsha followed by a motorcade about a mile long of chanting Old

Boys and admirers. The grandeur of the ceremony spoke volumes of the high esteem in which his former students held him.

In CKC academics was king, but a lot of premium was also put in sports because of the attributes of team work, determination and perseverance, physical and mental development and character formation that it promotes. The school won many trophies in both local and international competitions, the crowning example being the International School Sports Federation (ISSF) soccer trophy it won in Dublin in July 1977 when it beat Turkey on penalties after a 2-2 draw at full time. To reach the finals, it had beaten Luxembourg, France, Denmark, Finland and had drawn with the host Ireland. Rev. Fr. Fitzpatrick I am sure would have loved to be there. The college had also produced many engineers, medical doctors, eminent supreme court judges, university professors, and internationally acclaimed mathematicians to name a few.

We were all friends together really – obviously I was in so many teams that I was never short of companionship, but in secondary school my closest friends included Lambert Egbue and late Joe Ngene of blessed memories. Joe was not only brilliant but was a sports man par excellence. He was a bulwark of defence in our soccer team and the school champion in long jump. He died in a bomb air raid from Nigerian army during the Nigerian civil war. Our class was notable for the fiery but healthy competition in class work, but I always came among the first four in exams especially in our senior years.

The exceptionally brilliant in the class included James Okafor who finished top of the class in the West African School Certificate exam with A1 in eight subjects and graduated as a medical doctor in Germany, Gabriel Ejebe a first class graduate in electrical engineering with some patents to his name, Godfrey Ajah a graduate of mechanical engineering and a retired Permanent Secretary in Ebonyi State and Oliver Okonkwo alias Mobisson a graduate of Massachusetts Institute of Technology (MIT) and renowned computer engineer. Unfortunately, we lost Oliver in February 2010.

There were no girls at my school, but there was a sister school to ours, Queen of Rosary College (QRC) about 500 metres down the road. We mixed with the girls at big events such as sports day. As Catholics, some of us were selected to serve mass in the girl's school. I was used to female company because in my home village we had a Students Association for boys and girls and organised football or netball matches against other towns. We all met together for carol singing at the celebration of various festivals especially Christmas. I enjoyed the organised debates, too, and recall heated discussions when the subject was, 'this house believes that the coming of the white man has done more harm than good.' I particularly enjoyed democracy debates.

During my school years, I was influenced by some inspirational teachers. Mr Martin Okafor and Mr. Akudinobi, who were my maths teachers, gave me a love of the subject; Rev. Fr. Smith our Latin teacher who made Latin look easy and enjoyable; I remember him telling me before our West African School Certificate exam, 'Daniel if you don't get an A1 in Latin, don't talk to me!'. Unfortunately, I did disappoint him. I had A2. Mr Tony Osokolo brought humour into the classroom, making everybody feel relaxed. He was very motivational and masterful in the teaching of physics. As I considered my next steps concerning my choice of subject and university, I had to remember my next shot might be a new experience, but it could be the best shot I ever hit.

Christ the King College (CKC) Onitsha, 1961. I am in the back-row, sixth from the left

3

TRUSTING YOUR SWING

I t was an extremely proud moment for me and my family when I was accepted at Ahmadu Bello University in Zaria, North Central Nigeria, on a Federal Government Scholarship to study Mechanical Engineering. I had won the scholarship based on the results of my high school certificate exam. It had been a nerve-wracking time; I had applied to the university and anxiously awaited the acceptance letter, and the scholarship board contacted me by letter, informing me that I had been successful.

Mother was very excited but also apprehensive as to how much she would see of me. I had to trust my swing that I was making the right decision because I was only there for three months when I received a Special Commonwealth Aid to Africa Plan scholarship, known as SCAAP, and I made the decision to travel to Christchurch, New Zealand to enroll at the University of Canterbury. Looking back, this was probably one of the best decisions of my life, and I had done well to trust my swing.

It was the first time I had flown and the first time I had been abroad. It was exciting, a great honour and too good an opportunity to miss. The journey to New Zealand, even though I travelled alone, was very exciting. From Lagos we flew to Cairo where we spent two whole days waiting for the connecting flight to Bangkok, Thailand; then across the Indian Ocean to Perth in west Australia and then to Sydney from where finally we flew to Christchurch, New Zealand. In Cairo I experienced, first hand, the weather fluctuations of a desert country from extremely hot days to chilling cold nights. The flight across the Indian ocean did not provide any relaxation for me. It was long, about twelve hours. As an active outdoor bound young man, I had never had to sit in one place for that length of time. It was a big relief when we finally touched down in Perth. Despite the fact that I was so dreadfully homesick during the first three months, I gradually settled into my hostel accommodation at Warwick House, 52 Armagh Street, Christchurch. Unfortunately, it was later destroyed by an earthquake on Tuesday 22nd February 2011.

I lived in the hostel for two years, and then I stayed in a student house owned by an elderly widow from South Africa – we stayed on the ground floor, and she lived above. She was lovely to us and so welcoming. News from the grape vine had it that she and her husband had to leave South Africa under apartheid pressure as they were known to be open sympathisers of the Black nationalists who were fighting for independence. When her husband died in Australia, she relocated to New Zealand. We comforted her when she was so upset concerning the apartheid issues, and I recall we were living there when the South African prime minister, Hendrik Verwoerd, was stabbed to death.

Once I settled in, I was happy in Christchurch, a city in the South Island. It's known for its English heritage. It is a beautiful place where the Avon River meanders through the city centre. My university, the University of Canterbury, is New Zealand's second oldest university. It was founded in 1873 as Canterbury College, the first constituent college of the University of New Zealand. The main campus of the University was in the centre of town, but the engineering school was in the suburb called Illam.

I enjoyed sampling new foods, and my favourite New Zealand foods were lamb cutlets and the popular recipes containing fresh fish and prawns. It was in New Zealand that I first experienced the true meaning of winter, and I first witnessed snow. The frost was a huge shock, and after playing soccer, I was amazed how stiff my shoelaces and my fingers were! I couldn't undo my shoelaces, so I went home, filled the bath with very hot water and jumped in with my boots on! I later learnt that I was lucky not to develop chilblains. Central heating wasn't that common then and I invested in new warm nightclothes. One freezing day, when I was studying, I was practically sitting on the heater when I fell asleep and burnt my trousers!

I met a few other African students in the hostel and others from Malaysia, Vietnam and Singapore, so I soon made lots of friends, and I grew to enjoy my new life. I had some close friends. A Sri Lankan friend, Tissa Fernando, introduced me to many new dishes, such as sour fish curry, kottu and hoppers, and I enjoyed many a laugh with my Tanzanian friend, Hussein Mawona. In fact, I am still in touch with Tissa and we communicate a lot by email and the messenger apps. I appreciate the many photos of our friends he forwards to me, and he told me the whereabouts of other friends I had lost contact with – Merton Tapp and Don Richards – and he told me about all their news.

Tissa was always absolutely crazy about cricket and used to stay up all night listening to the radio reports of Sri Lanka playing England at the Oval. He slept in a bunk above my bed, and during one of his all-nighters, he fell from his bunk above me. I was not too amused by the fact he could have killed me, but actually I did nearly kill myself with laughter! My Malaysian friend, Anuar bin Khalid, was from a wealthy family, and he owned a car, which was a most unusual possession for first year student in those days! He also studied engineering and would drive me to the school at Ilam. We respected each other's religions; he was a Muslim, and I was a Christian. We usually got on together extremely well, but one day Anuar was praying in his room, and I went in shouting. He was very angry with me and didn't speak for about two days!

Life in the hostel was a lot of fun as could be expected in any gathering of young men, with noisy parties, music and dancing almost every weekend. The live wire of the parties in my first year in the hostel was a Maori student, Monty Ohai, in whose presence you didn't have a choice but to be happy. He was a good guitarist and would entertain us with music and jokes. Unfortunately, Monty did not come back to the university after end of the year holidays. We missed him but we were not very surprised. He told us after each of the past two holidays that his mates back home were laughing at him for wasting his time in university when he could be making tons of money working in freezing factories loading lamb carcasses.

Another student who did not come back was sadly the hostel president R B Cole. The vivacious youth with ever friendly disposition had gone skiing in stormy waters when a huge wave washed him away and his corpse was never recovered. In fact, it was not unusual for many students to come back from the long vacations in plaster as a result of accidents sustained either from snow skiing, water skiing or mountain hiking. As a result of these apparently frequent accidents, I turned down all invitations to participate in these three sports. I decided to stick with what I knew best. This was soccer and tennis, even though I tried my hand with hitting golf balls at the range a couple of times.

My only encounter with any sea sports was after graduation when I accompanied my Student Officer Rhys

WARWICK HOUSE
- 1965 -
UNIVERSITY OF CANTERBURY

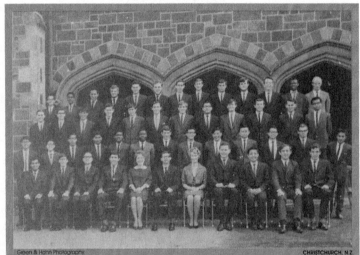

Green & Hahn Photography   CHRISTCHURCH, N.Z.

Back Row: C. Y. Yew, L.Abdul, M. R. Ohia, P. F. Davis, K. N. Martin, W. F. C. Taylor, J. G. Sinclair, I. C . Whiteford, R. W. G. Blakeley, M. R. Tapp, G. R. Wrigley, D. O. Chuke, B. E. De Ridder.

Third Row: B. M. Peake, P. R. Ireland, M. J. Major, P. J. Cameron, D. Steven, I . F. Cull, J. R. Rutherford, C. O. Fong, F. C. March, H. J. N. Duckworth, P. D. Lucas, A. B. Kadis.

Second Row: N. T. Son, T. P. Tuong, T. M. Ismail, M. Shanmugan, T. Fernando, H. Mawona, F. J. Fairweather, F. J Chin, M. Chan, P. Leophairatana, S. Y. Chang, N. R. Nicholls, M. A. Khalid.

Front Row: M. Yunus Noor (Junior Fellow), P. L. Campbell (Committee), E. S. Tan (Treasurer), R. B. Cole (President), Mrs L. F. Phillips, Dr. L. F. Phillips (Warden).

Absent: C. G. Moore (Vice-President).

Housemen for part of 1965: J. K. W. Isles (Committee), T. E. Robson.

Richards to spend Christmas vacation at his brother Lyn Richard's house in a rural coastal town in the northeast of the country. Lyn Richards had lived in Nigeria, teaching at Mayflower School Ikenne in Western Nigeria. We would take a speed boat about one hundred metres into the sea to cast our net for crayfish. One day on our way back to the shore two of us decided to jump out of the boat and swim the rest of the distance. When I thought we were close enough, I went down hoping to touch ground only to find to my chagrin that the water depth was still about twice my height. I reached up and tiredly plodded the rest of the distance to land very exhausted and frankly very scared. I never tried it again. The rest of the holidays went very well. We enjoyed the country style New Year's Eve celebration dancing the poker till the wee hours of the morning.

I studied mechanical engineering, which I found to be a very interesting course. We actually had a departmental computer, but they were still very new inventions; it was a huge giant thing that filled the room. We had to use punch cards for input and output of data. The teacher, Mr. Moon, was not very inspiring – a stiff fellow who bored us all with his monotone voice and lack of enthusiasm, so none of his students made much progress concerning computer studies. However, we all loved the thermo-dynamics & heat engines classes plus the practical side of our subject in the labs. Prof. H T Adams, the deputy dean of engineering, was one of the tutors who motivated us with his engrossing and informative lectures.

During the long vacations, we went to factories to gain work experience. On one such occasion I acquired a vacation job in Upper Hutt, a town north of Wellington. I travelled by train and had to get there by 9 a.m. although we could start as early as 6 a.m. From 6 to 8 a.m., we would receive double pay, and from 8.30 to 9 a.m., we would be on one and a half pay, so naturally we tried to get there as early as possible in order to gain the extra money. One day I fell asleep on the train and missed my stop. The conductor looked at my ticket, and he said I'd passed the stop an hour ago! I eventually arrived at work at 11 a.m. instead of 6 or 8 a.m., so in place of a bonus I was heavily penalised! There is a waterfront promenade in Wellington, sandy beaches, a harbour and colourful timber houses on surrounding hills.

I thoroughly appreciated seeing more of this beautiful island country in the southwestern Pacific Ocean. It consists of two main landmasses – the North Island and the South Island plus over 600 smaller islands, covering a total of 268,021 square kilometres. I enjoyed learning about the indigenous Maori culture, and of course, I had to see a kiwi, the unofficial national emblem. It is a curious tailless bird, which cannot fly. New Zealanders are nicknamed 'kiwis', and they made me very welcome during my six years there. My stay in New Zealand was the chance of a lifetime to experience mountain vistas, ancient forests, volcanic landscapes, stunning coastlines and unique wildlife encounters.

There were opportunities for whale watching, dolphin encounters and bird watching. Blue penguins are found right around the coast of New Zealand. The royal albatrosses were magnificent large birds with their three-metre wingspan! Amidst New Zealand's caves, grottos and native forests, you can discover glow worms. Thousands of these tiny creatures can light up a cave roof. We could spot them on the banks of some lakes and in damp, overgrown habitats.

I travelled as much as time and finances would permit during my vacations. I also joined the African Society, and we went on a great trip to Dunedin on the South Island's southeast coast. The landscape was dramatic with the adjoining Otago peninsula, home to the colonies of albatrosses and penguins I already mentioned. Dunedin has the steepest road in the world, with a slope of 19 degrees. One Okoronkwo Okereke, a Nigerian student at Lincoln College of Agriculture, and I also took a trip around most of Northern Island of New Zealand, travelling along the east coast from Wellington to Hastings, Napier, Gisborne, then across to Rotorua coming back to Wellington through New Plymouth to Palmerston North on the west coast.

Rotorua was breath-takingly rewarding with nature at some of its most mind boggling. Hot spring water with the aroma of minerals including sulphur was oozing out of the ground and the scattered lakes. The spring water was reputed to have health renewing properties and to cure ailments like arthritis, skin diseases and joint pains. They are also relaxing; we were privileged to bathe in the hot springs. The trip was adventurous in that we slept in our car in open holiday parks without any worries about security. Unfortunately, I understand that security has become a big issue now as in many parts of the world. In addition, we enjoyed taking an overnight trip on a boat from Christchurch to Wellington and vice versa, arriving early in the morning.

In May 1968 when I was still living in Christchurch, an earthquake was felt one early morning about 5.30 am. I was still in bed and all of a sudden, my bed seemed to be oscillating violently from one end of the room to the other. It may have lasted less than one minute that seemed like eternity. Later in the day we learnt that the epicentre was at a sparsely populated community called Inangahua in the northern South Island. I still shudder with fear when I remember the 2011 earthquake that caused so much destruction of life and property in Christchurch. Boy was I lucky!

We grew to accept the colder weather. New Zealand's climate varies wildly - the far north has subtropical weather during summer, while inland alpine areas of the South Island can be as cold as minus 10. However, most of the country lies close to the coast, which means mild temperatures all year round.

My university days mirrored my school days in the fact

I spent many hours playing soccer, and I was selected to play for the combined team of the six universities, which the country had at that time. I have played soccer matches all over beautiful New Zealand. Of course, I reveled in all the accompanying beer drinking, and I became a fan of rugby too, participating fully in all the rugby songs on our match journeys' return home. The interaction after any of our sporting activities, of so many young men going to the bar together, was the perfect finish to any game. Whatever the score – because we could drown our sorrows or celebrate our victory! There were three Africans on this team, two Nigerians, Raymond Nwaokobia and myself, with Mori Lamin coming from Sierra Leone. Only the Vice Captain Terry McKain and I made the cut from the University of Canterbury.

Occasionally I attended the horse racing in Christchurch. A group of us might go to the racecourse, but remember, we were not well off, so there was little chance of us students becoming addicted to gambling away the fortunes we did not have! I did place the odd bet and savoured the thrill of a win. It was just another light-hearted way to spend leisure time together as a group of boys. There was a university international club, of which I was a member. We would take it in turns to host the meetings, appreciating the many opportunities to meet people from all over the world. It was such a good opportunity to make new friends and to overcome any barriers of language, culture or religion.

I qualified with a Bachelor of Engineering in 1967, and I still recall the roof-shaking ovation I received when my name was called to receive my diploma at the graduation ceremony even though no relatives of mine were present. In 1968 I gained my postgraduate degree in business administration, which assisted me greatly by further developing my interpersonal and communication skills plus collaborative learning. I felt ready to face a fast-paced professional environment. It had taught me the necessity of not just focusing on one part of an organisation. I knew now how to oversee different business operations, ranging from marketing to finance. I was able to understand marketing and accounting principles, economics and finance and global business strategies, and I had some insight into law and ethics.

The ability to analyse data and market trends was to prove very helpful as my career progressed. I knew that, armed with my qualification in business administration, I could work in a variety of sectors. I now knew that placing the ball in the right position for the next shot was an essential move, as I considered my employment options.

NEW ZEALAND UNIVERSITIES ASSOCIATION FOOTBALL TEAM

Representative Touring Side - 1968

Standing: M. A. PETERS   R. H. HOWELL   A. R. MUDFORD   G. GRINLAUBS   D. O. CHUKE   M. E. S. LAMIN   K. J. DAVEY

Sitting: R. N. NWAOKOBIA   K. P. TOO   J. A. LAWRENCE (Captain)   R. A. BUSTARD (Manager)   C. T. McKAIN (Vice-Captain)   R. M. LINGARD

Absent: S. KARDOS   E. TELENI

Frank Thompson, Crown Studios, Wellington.

University of Canterbury, Mechanical Engineering class of 1967

Graduation, 1967

4

BIRDIE, EAGLE, ALBATROSS OR CONDOR

Things had gone well at university. I felt I had often scored under par in all I had achieved. Golf is a game of confidence, and my confidence had grown so much during those university years. One regret, however, was that my family were never able to visit me, and I couldn't go home for six years; four of those were at university and a further two as I found my feet in the world of work. The Nigerian Civil War struck in July 1967 and lasted until 15th January 1970, so obviously this had a huge impact on me by making it impossible for me to see my family. It was also known as the Nigerian Biafran War or the Biafran War.

It was a civil war fought between the government of Nigeria and the Republic of Biafra, which was forced to declare its independence from Nigeria in 1967 as a result of the most bestial and barbaric pogrom against its people by the Nigerian government with the full support of Prime Minister Harold Wilson of Britain. My brother was in the United States, working as a doctor, so I managed to communicate with him to discover the welfare of my mother. It was incredibly difficult to communicate with home, so I tried every channel I could think of; my sister was married to the ambassador of Biafra in East Africa, so I discovered that I could keep in touch with her and with my other sister, who was based in London, to get any inkling of what was happening at home.

The evening news on New Zealand television was dreadful to watch because any news on Biafra featured children with distended stomachs said to be suffering from kwashiorkor as a result of malnutrition. It was naturally a very worrying and distressing time because I could go for months without any contact with my family. Some of my good friends were killed. UNICEF and other agencies were helping with aid - the Biafran Airlift was an international humanitarian relief effort that transported food and medicine to Biafra during the war. The airlift was largely a series of joint efforts by Catholic and Protestant church groups and other non-governmental organisations (NGOs) operating civilian and military aircraft with volunteer civilian crews and support personnel. Caritas, a Catholic charity, supplied dried milk, corned beef, salt and egg yolk to the millions suffering acute hunger.

Staying in New Zealand, I applied in Wellington for a building services position as a design engineer with the New Zealand Ministry of Works. This was in 1968, and I was proud of my position as assistant engineer in the Building Services Department where I designed air-conditioning, ventilation and plumbing systems of high rise and large industrial and commercial buildings. I worked for Frank Blackwell, a very nice man who was an inspiration to me in future years regarding my own staff relationships with junior members. In our team were, amongst others, two of my classmates from University of Canterbury, John Hunter and Ian Leask.

I found accommodation with two guys, one from Malawi and one from Nigeria. I remained in that job for two years; they wanted me to stay on, but I was itching to go home. I knew I still couldn't make it back to Nigeria as the war was just ending, and there was uncertainty regarding security and employment opportunities, but by then my brother was in Zambia working as a professor of medicine and President Kaunda's personal physician. I therefore decided to head to Zambia as a first stage of my return home.

I initially was offered work at the copper mines with a condition that I had to start in the pit, 200 metres underground where I would repair and maintain engineering and service equipment. This is quite normal and indeed is the fastest way a young engineer would familiarise himself with the mining process. I knew I would eventually go back to Nigeria. What was most important to me was to acquire skills I could transfer home with comparative advantage. Although we had coal mines in Enugu, being a coal miner did not particularly appeal to me as a career, so I turned down the offer and applied for other jobs.

My dream employment came in Lusaka as a project officer in the Industrial Development Corporation, known as INDECO. I commenced the post in 1971, and I had to conduct feasibility studies for new industries in order to establish their technical and commercial viability and also participated in their project management if the company decided to proceed with their development. Indeco was the Zambian Government vehicle for participating in the industrialisation of the country.

Apart from establishing new manufacturing companies, it also took majority shares in already running strategic industries owned by expatriates. Zambia wanted a larger role in the management and ownership of key industries after its independence. To this extent, when manganese oxide, a key component raw material for dry cell production, was discovered in Mansa, Luapula Province, I conducted a feasibility study to determine the viability of manufacturing dry cell batteries in Mansa. The study indicated positive results and we selected Oy Airam of Finland as joint venture partners. I became the project manager responsible for the project implementation. This involved considerable travelling to the various machinery vendors to agree on specifications and expedite delivery so that time schedules could be met.

The project included, apart from the construction of the

factory, a residential complex with all the services in place. Mansa was a rural community without any accommodation for the staff. We also had to train technicians to operate the factory. I had earlier performed similar project management duties in the setup of the Fiat vehicle assembly plant in Livingstone, a town on the border with Zimbabwe. Livingstone is famous for waterfalls called Livingstone Water Falls or Mosi-o-tunya in local dialect which translates to The Smoke that Thunders. You can hear the noise from the falls from far away and the mist that forms as the water hits the rock at the bottom of the falls fills the air. It is a UNESCO World Heritage Centre and a marvel to behold, a tourist attraction. I have been there numerous times as the site is just behind the Hotel that bears its name, Mosi-o-tunya hotel where I stayed during my numerous visits to Livingstone during the factory construction and subsequent board meetings. Many extra driven adventurers have lost their lives climbing down to the bottom of the Falls.

Because I travelled a lot with work, I was provided with a Fiat 132 car on a discount. I had first learnt to drive in New Zealand, and two years after arrival I had bought an old Ford Prefect. At weekends, I used to drive to Brighton, a small seaside town within the city limits of Christchurch. We had great fun because the town faces a small bay, which includes a broad, sheltered beach. I had a Scottish friend, and every time I needed my car fixed, he repaired it for me. He kept patching it up, but after a year, I sold it to a car wrecker who laughed at the state of it and offered me just 27 dollars, which I took although I had paid 270 dollars for it originally. I then bought a Volkswagen Beetle.

The Executive Chairman CEO Indeco Elias Andrew Kashita, fondly called EAK, was the first Zambian to qualify as mechanical engineer, a brilliant and humorous man and a keen squash player who graduated from University of Reading in UK. Even though I was not a Zambian, it did not take him long to start assigning to me important responsibilities in the company. We travelled extensively together for business negotiations. Indeco had at that time over 72 subsidiary companies and to facilitate effective management and control was grouped into six sub holding companies each headed by a Managing Director who reported to the Chairman. I was in the Project Development department at the head office. I recall one long trip we went on together. It was exciting as we went to Rome, Milan, Florence, Turin, Venice, then the United States and Edmonton in Canada before crossing the International date line to Sweden, Finland from where we spent some time in London and Isle of Man. I suppose it might be fair to say we did a mini world tour!

I particularly enjoyed my time in Orlando. I will never forget the Hall of the Presidents, an attraction located in Liberty Square at the Magic Kingdom. Thirty-seven presidents of the US are housed in a building created to look like Philadelphia's Independence Hall. The Presidents appear in an audio-animatronic form. Venice offered something unique, a city without roads which were replaced with water channels and the only means of movement within the city was by small boats called gondolas. The only land I recall seeing was around St. Michael's Square. We stayed at the luxurious Hotel Danieli which is reputed for hosting Hollywood celebrities; why not, we were guests of ENI group. I marveled at the construction of the city but privately pondered its sustainability. It seemed to me that the city was sinking slowly as the water level was slowly approaching the door level of most houses. In Florence we saw the house where Leonardo da Vinci spent his early days of apprenticeship.

During this post, I represented Indeco on the boards of many companies in which the company has financial interest. I dipped my toes into boardroom politics and management for the first time, gaining a valuable foundation for my future careers. I also went to Egypt to discuss cooperation in industrial development between the two countries, especially where the use of copper could play a significant role. I managed to fit in a tour to see the pyramids. Incidentally, it was the period the exhibition of the famous Tutankhamun was showing at the Cairo Museum. Tutankhamun was a boy pharaoh who ascended the throne in 1332 BC at the age of ten and ruled for nine years. His tomb and treasures were discovered and excavated in a monumental discovery which shook the world October 1925 by a British archaeologist Edward Carter.

The tomb consisted of concentric caskets from the innermost which was of solid gold where the pharaoh was laid, the immediate outer one also where his fabulous treasures of gold and precious stones were stored, was also in gold. The other outer caskets were of wood and glass. The amazing thing was that after almost 2000 years after burial the body of the pharaoh was intact. I marveled at the technology the Egyptians must have had that enabled them to perform such feats.

We also visited the pyramid of Giza to behold the engineering feat performed by the ancient Egyptians. One of the three main pyramids in the site, named the Great Pyramid, we were told, was 200m square at the base and also 200 metres high, built with stone cubes each weighing one ton. The stone cubes were hauled up the Nile river from the quarry from the south and stacked up one on top of the other to create the pyramid, making provision for the chambers inside. How these stone cubes were cut to exact size and weight, transported up the river using what vessels, stacked up to form a pyramid and create the void almost two thousand years ago was completely baffling to me. They must have enjoyed a level of civilization and engineering proficiency well beyond their time. Why did the development not progress, I wondered! I grew to love Egyptian coffee which is so thick that you can literally chew it, so I ensured that I brought supplies back!

My career had rapidly taken off. I had started off well, kept out of the rough, and having seen so much of the world in such a short space of time, I think it is fair to say my game was going well!

Our wedding day: Toasting my beautiful bride, Ezim.
Saturday 22nd February, 1975

Our wedding day: My elder brother, Prof. Paul Chuke standing first on the left

My wife and I being received by the British High Commissioner

With Professor Chike Edozien (Asagba of Asaba) at CKC Old Boys Reception

With businessman, Sir Emeka Offor (Sir E)

5

IMPROVING MY HANDICAP

I read somewhere that 80% of golfers will never achieve a handicap of less than 18! Such figures do not bother me because I don't pace myself by the achievements of others. One has to aim high, regardless of the predictions of others.

In 1976 I returned to Nigeria, where I worked as project manager at the Central Investment Company in Enugu, Eastern Nigeria. The functions and objectives were somehow similar to those of Indeco in Zambia but on a much smaller scale. I had therefore achieved my projected aim, to acquire skill I could transfer home with comparative advantage; so, I hit the ground running. I was promoted General Manager and CEO of the company within three years when the incumbent retired.

I helped the government and private entrepreneurs to establish manufacturing industries by preparing feasibility studies and providing project financing and project management. The scope of our mandate extended as well to rehabilitation of ailing industries. Under my watch, we established Premier Breweries and Life Brewery both in Onitsha, the first for the government and the later for a consortium of private shareholders. From 1979 I was the general manager and CEO until I left in 1983. I represented the company on the Council of the Nigerian Stock Exchange and Board of the National Science and Technology Fund.

I was also on the board of many companies like Premier Breweries and Life Brewery, Niger Steel amongst others where the experience I gained in Indeco helped me extensively. I travelled widely too with my new job to the UK, France, Malaysia, Singapore and Kingston Jamaica. On one of my business trips to Lagos I decided to pay a courtesy visit to the Communication Bureau of the US Embassy where a US Embassy Staff, Arthur Lewis, I had met in Zambia had been transferred. During our conversation, he informed me of a programme they were running, awarding a travel visit to promising Nigerian leaders to the USA, and urged me to apply. I did and got the award. So, in 1978 I embarked on a seven-week tour of the USA sponsored by the embassy.

In Washington a tour guide was assigned to me, and we toured Washington, New Orleans, Los Angeles including Disneyland, Chicago with Sears Tower and Kansas City. I found Washington quite intimidating; the expansive green fields and landscaping of the Washington Memorial and Jefferson Memorial, the massive structures of buildings like the Watergate Complex, though there were no high-rise buildings. We climbed Sears Tower now called Willis

Tower, the then-tallest building in the world, and from the observation deck saw all of Chicago and beyond, a bewildering experience for anyone who had never seen any building higher than ten stories. Sears tower is 108 stories, 1450 ft high.

My most impressive experience was to come in Disneyland with an encounter in exhibition titled 'A Meeting with Mr. President'. Everybody was seated in the studio hall and the window curtains closed. Slowly the stage curtains started to open and sitting by the table was the life size of Abraham Lincoln who stood up slowly and gracefully delivered a powerful speech. The stage curtains once again closed, and lights switched on. The effect on me was stunning. I was dazed beyond belief. I sat in my chair not able or willing to get up and leave like the others. I had never seen or imagined anything like that before. What could technology not achieve? I returned to Nigeria fully energised and dreaming of the wide possibilities life can offer.

As my rank improved, so did my house! I lived in a flat until I became the controller of operations and soon after the general manager of the company, when I moved with my family into a grand five-bedroomed house with a large garden. The house had two beautiful sitting rooms plus boys' quarters and a magnificent guest house.

I decided to retire from the company in 1983 and started my own business, becoming an industrial management consultant with Otago Nig Ltd, which I created. I continued in the line of business I had engaged in since my days in Zambia. It was then that the Federal Government of Nigeria decided to ban the importation of malted barley, the key ingredient raw material in beer brewing thus forcing local manufacturers to find alternative replacement. Breweries and universities researched on it, trying many local materials like maize, cassava and sorghum either alone or in combination. Finally malted sorghum was adopted as the most advantageous alternative. However malted sorghum did not have enough indigenous enzymes needed for best result in fermentation and other brewing processes making it mandatory that external enzymes be introduced.

Working with universities, I conducted seminars and workshops to externalise the results of the research and teach brewers what must now be done. In addition, I discovered an enzyme manufacturer in France, Gist Brocades of Seclin near Lille, who were only too happy for me to represent them on the Nigerian vast market; I got involved with brewing materials and supplies.

I consulted for the private sector as well working with the company leadership to assess the company and identify problems, gather information and implement solutions with the collaboration when so needed with other engineers. So it was that engineer Roy Umenyi, Dr. Sam Chukwujekwu and I worked together in the rehabilitation of Ihiala Starch Mills. My aim was to help companies succeed in the vast opportunities, both internationally and locally. I strived to take business to the next level with my tailored services, so, once again, I often lived out of a suitcase due to all the necessary business travel. I would conduct research of the markets, investment potential and logistics optimisation. I was in Seclin many times travelling to Lille through London on the EuroStar and by taxi to Seclin, or through Paris and by rail from Gare-du-Nord station to Lille. I had the opportunity to see a lot of the French countryside from the moving train. Every piece of land was either actively engaged in farming, crop and animal husbandry or planned forest reserve. I marveled at the maximum utilisation of their land assets.

Additionally, I was elected president of the Enugu Chamber of Commerce, Industry, Mines and Agriculture (ECCIMA) from 1987 to 1991, which meant that I was on the Council of the Nigerian Association of Chambers of Commerce Industry, Mines and Agriculture (NACCIMA). At ECCIMA, we associated closely with NASENI (National Agency for Science and Engineering Infrastructure), which was established in 1992 by the Federal Government as a parastatal of the Ministry of Science & Technology. Engineering departments of universities, especially University of Nigeria Nsukka, were developing prototypes for the production of tools and equipment, and in ECCIMA we strove to attract the private sector to convert these research results and prototypes into commercial production.

The National Agency for Science and Engineering

Infrastructure (NASENI) was also very active in this area and we collaborated effectively with them. I have always firmly believed that Nigeria could never develop unless we took the fundamental issues of development by the horn and NASENI was making giant and commendable efforts in this direction. It was therefore fortuitous that several years later when I became Minister, a memo for the dissolution of NASENI was brought to the cabinet council. Armed with my knowledge of the important role of the agency in promoting industrialisation, I had no option but to fight against the proposition especially since I was alerted to expect the memo by Dr Timothy Obiaga, a director in the Ministry of Science and Technology in the morning before the Council Meeting; we succeeded in stopping NASENI from going under the hammer. I am quite proud of my role. Under my watch, NACCIMA organised and hosted the first international trade fair south of the Niger and Benue rivers. It was a huge success and was officially opened by President Ibrahim Babangida.

I became involved with politics when I was about 55. I ran for the Federal House of Representatives and actually won the primary election under the platform of the Peoples Democratic Party, PDP. Before the elections however, my opponents wrote an anonymous and malicious petition falsely accusing me of being a member of NADECO, an organisation strongly opposed and committed to the downfall of the Head of State General Abacha. So it was that my name was removed from the list of those qualified to stand for election.

Fortuitously, General Abacha mysteriously died before the scheduled date of the election and his successor cancelled it per se. President, Olusegun Obasanjo, on assumption of office in 1999, after assessing my portfolio, appointed me Minister of Special Projects and in 2021 transferred me to the ministry of Defence as Minister of Defence responsible for the Air Force. As a minister I attended the Federal Executive Council meetings as a member of the cabinet, which meetings held each Wednesday from 10 a.m. until 2 p.m. at the State House in Abuja.

As Minister of Special Projects, I was involved in the Niger Delta Project. I was so interested in organising sustainable, people-centred development goals in the area. The position was so unique that I wanted to help with redevelopment, linking policy with planning and programming by instating quality social and environmental safeguards. The Niger Delta region covered nine states and all of them suffered in unequal degrees from the negative effects associated with oil exploration, production and refining which include but are not limited to environmental pollution, coastal erosion and destruction of aquatic life and farmlands. We called for proposals for a master plan that will ensure holistic development and we created the Niger Delta Development Corporation, NNDC, to take over the assets and liabilities of the defunct OMPADEC and hopefully succeed where the latter so woefully failed.

I went on a tour of oil-bearing communities in the Niger

Delta and promised that the proposed NDDC would remove the constraints that made it difficult for the defunct Oil Minerals Producing and Development Commission to meet the aspirations of the people. The aim of all my travel was to assess by first-hand encounters and acquaint myself with all the problems the communities have been facing. Apart from environmental pollution and degradation mentioned earlier was the problem created by gas flaring which turned nights into days. Gas flaring is the burning of natural gas associated with oil extraction. It is a method of disposing of the associated gas from oil production, but it is seen as a waste of a valuable natural resource.

There were so many opportunities to redevelop the world's second largest delta for tourism, and as a magnet for nature lovers, with the beautiful rivers and their oxbow lakes and meander belts, the magnificent scenery and the mangroves. It is the home of the world's largest diversity of butterflies, countless species of flora and terrestrial and aquatic fauna. We hoped a master plan will take all these aspects into consideration, such as how to successfully manage the coastal groundwater and climate of heavy rainfall, water supplies from bore holes or desalination of seawater, the manufacturing of water pipes and sanitation of some coastal communities. There were so many issues to consider, from the erection of more hospitals to noise levels and fears that independent fishing had been spoiled and farms destroyed by the oil spills. There were issues of air pollution causing serious destruction of the biodiversity of the Niger Delta.

We succeeded in establishing the Niger Delta Commission that working with the report of the master plan will offer lasting solutions to all these socio-economic difficulties. However, the lack of political will aborted the master plan project. I did however prepare a road map for the NNDC which I know has helped it in charting its route towards developing the region into a socially stable, politically peaceful and ecologically regenerated region that can be economically prosperous.

My position as Minister of Defence involved the management of the air force of the Federal Republic of Nigeria to ensure a professional force for the protection of the national territory. I was responsible for issues of airspace and for the connected security interests of the country.

My responsibilities included further travel to the United Kingdom, Italy, Russia, Indonesia and China, where we trained staff and sourced equipment and materials. In Russia I toured Moscow factories wearing my hat of Minister of Defence and enjoyed the thrill of flying an aircraft in a simulator without leaving the ground. In China I discussed matters with CATIC – the China National Aero- Technology Import and Export Corporation. It was the first state-owned corporation approved by the State Council of China as the state authorised dealer of defence products and technology. CATIC provides defence and security to the Chinese Air

Force. In Italy I discussed the training with the Italian Air Force, supply of needed platforms and rehabilitation of those in service. I was impressed by the advances Indonesia and the Asian Tiger nations have made in aero technology.

In Paris it was extremely interesting to visit the air show. It offered an opportunity to see all aircraft and related equipment vendors in one arena to discuss new and ongoing business. The dog fight demonstration by two fighter jets was the climax, the two pilots making incredible acrobatic displays with their fighter jets, diving, rotating, flying belly up or with the wings perpendicular to the ground. It was simply breathtaking. I took the opportunity to visit the Notre Dame cathedral where the Crown of Thorns which the Jews forced on the head of Jesus Christ is domiciled. In fact, I happened to be in the cathedral on a Wednesday at about 3.00 p.m. when the famous Crown of Thorns was being venerated; I was privileged to participate. The cathedral took 182 years to build starting from the year 1163. I had dinner on a tourist boat as it cruised along the Seine River showing the great places of interest in Paris.

Wherever I travelled, I tried to learn a few choice phrases in the native languages so that I could introduce myself and make a few appropriate comments. I felt that it was a sign of respect to my hosts to at least attempt to say a few words in their language.

I thoroughly enjoyed my career, and I feel I achieved much for the nation, for myself and my family. I reckon if my career had in fact been a game of golf, I would have been very content with the score and my resulting handicap!

With President Ibrahim Babangida at the opening of First Enugu Internatiĩnal Trade Fair.

Receiving President Olusegun Obasanjo, from left: Chief of Defence, Admiral Oogohi; Minister of Airforce, Dan Chuke; Minister of Navy, Dupe Adelaja; Minister of Army, Lawal Batagarawa.

Male Ministers from South East, from left: ABC Nwosu, Dan Chuke, Ojo Maduekwe, Tim Menakaya, Vin Ogbulafor.

Visit to Airforce Training School, South Italy

With two former Nigerian Presidents, Alh. Shehu Shagari ad Gen. Yakuba Gowon.

Signing a Memorandum in Beijing, China

With the Chinese Minister of Defence

With Secretary to the Government of the Federation (SGF), Ufot Ekaete

With Gen T.Y Danjuma and the Chinese Ambassador to Nigeria

With the Chief of Air Staff at Agusta Helicopter Plant in Italy

Making a speech at Airforce rifle shooting training

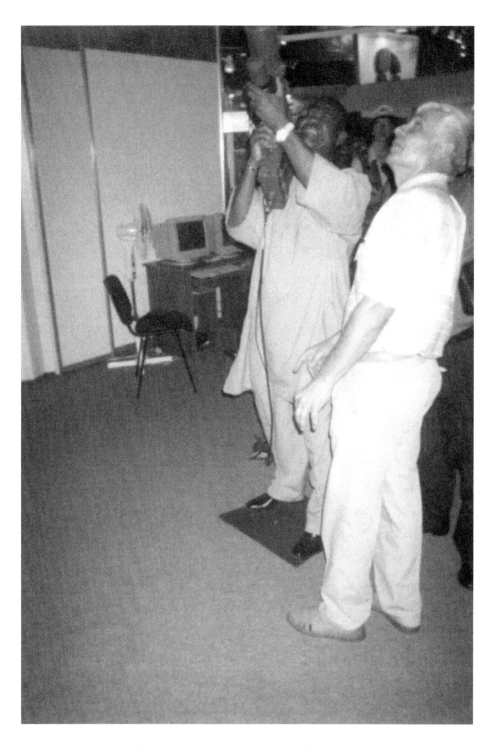

Having a feel at firing surface to air missile in Moscow

6

THE ACE

was living and working in Zambia, but in 1973, I finally travelled home to Nigeria to attend my immediate elder brother Bon's wedding. I had decided to extend my stay as a holiday, catching up with family and friends. I scored an ace as it turned out to be the best holiday of my lifetime because I won the best trophy in the world when Florence Ezim Obionwu became my devoted, caring wife in 1975. I was 32 years old, and mutual friends had introduced us on my return to our village. I liked her style, and I guess she liked mine, and the rest is history!

Mum was happy for us, and she knew Florence's grandmother, so there was an immediate connection. Our wedding took place in Zambia. I wore black, and Florence looked stunning in her traditional white dress. I will never forget my feelings of pride and love as my beautiful bride entered the church to the wedding march by Richard Wagner. I will always remember 'Here Comes the Bride' as my dear wife-to-be approached me.

Unfortunately, my mum couldn't come to the wedding. However, my elder brother Paul, a professor and medical physician, supported me, accompanied by his young children, Onyema, Emeka and baby Chidi. His wife Lily was then in London for a short study course. My boss, Andrew Elias Kashita, also attended with his wife, Margaret. Our many Nigerian friends who lived nearby joined in the extremely happy celebrations at our dinner dance reception. It rained as the reception ended, which is recognised as a good omen for a happy marriage; this has certainly been the case because in 2025 we will celebrate our golden wedding anniversary. Our wedding day was perfect, and neither of us minded that there was no honeymoon and that we were back to work on Monday.

My wife, Lady Florence, has studied at Evelyn Hone College in Lusaka; Pitman's College, London; and the Enugu State University of Technology (ESUT), where she was awarded a master's degree in public administration. An accomplished civil servant, she eventually retired as director of administration in the Anambra State Government. Florence is a successful leader in her own right and had held the position of President of the Anambra State Trefoil Guild for 10 years. When I travelled from Nigeria on business trips, Florence sometimes accompanied me, and we enjoyed the advantage of being able to spend time together in China, the United Kingdom and Russia when I was working as the Minister of Defence with the air force, and Florence would be provided with an escort to show her the sights while I was in business meetings, but, of course, we would meet up for evening dinners and shows.

We had commenced our married life living in a flat owned by my company, and it was a huge blessing when our first child, Ify Diana, was born in Zambia in March 1976. We left Zambia in October of that year because we wanted to move closer to our family and our roots. After living so far away in New Zealand, it was such a joy for me to now live just an hour's drive from Mum in our three-bedroomed, first floor flat. Ify settled into her nursery and was delighted to become a big sister to Chidubem Daniel in 1978. Florence and I were blessed with two more children, Chiamaka Vanessa in 1979 and Kenechukwu Michael in 1982.

We raised our children in similar ways to our own upbringing and gave each, small chores, for example, washing the plates after meals. We employed a nanny when Florence worked. When we occasionally travelled abroad together with my work, Florence would look after our children. When the children were older, during secondary school years, they joined us when they were home from their boarding schools. During some vacations, usually at Christmas and Easter times, we ensured that our children experienced village life by going to the village with them.

Florence and I loved to be active in the lives of our children; I played tennis with my sons and Florence introduced the girls to guiding and became the chairperson of Trefoil guiding for the state. As a family, we all attended church every Sunday, and the religious rites of passage were faithfully celebrated.

Our children have brought us nothing but joy and pride, and we are eternally thankful to God for our magnificent brood. While Ify was educated at the high-ranking Queen's School, Enugu, Chiamaka attended the equally prestigious Catholic Holy Rosary Secondary School, also in Enugu, where she was the senior prefect in her final year. Chidubem attended the well-regarded Jesuit's secondary school in Uturu, Okigwe for the first three years and had to relocate to the highly competitive federal government school in Enugu for health reasons. Kenechukwu had his education at the well-staffed University Secondary School, also in Enugu.

Florence and I offered our children a free choice of careers but insisted that they should earn their first degrees in Nigeria to give them the opportunity to make local friendships. We guided them by suggesting relevant considerations before asking them to make their own choices for their postgraduate studies. Therefore, all our children studied in Nigeria for their first degrees, although Ify had to leave for the United States during her undergraduate year because a one-year academic staff strike paralysed all Nigerian universities in 1996. She studied economics at the Wesleyan University, where she was an Etherington scholar. She then capped her studies with law at the New York Law School.

Chidubem and Chiamaka both studied computer science and information technology at the Federal University of Technology (FUTO), Owerri, and the Nnamdi Azikiwe University of Technology, Awka, respectively, before going to the United Kingdom, where they completed their master's degrees. Chidubem studied at the University of Greenwich and achieved a merit award, and Chiamaka studied at the University of Cardiff, gaining a distinction. Kenechukwu studied business administration at the University of Abuja.

Ify, with her versatile background in economics and law, opted to go into business. She founded and is the CEO of Miracle in the Green, a leading moringa brand, which manufactures health and wellness products. Her baby skincare, household and beauty products have been featured in top magazines in Europe and America and sold in several countries. A brave young lady and a breast cancer survivor, on her own, she withdrew herself from further chemotherapy and opted for alternative treatment. She has been cancer free for over 10 years now. Ify is married to Dr Obinna Nwobi, a vascular surgeon, and they live in the United States with their four children.

Chidubem is a leukaemia survivor. He has been through very trying times, but his zest for life, determination plus tremendous developments in medicine (along with the intervention of the Almighty God) have put smiles on our faces. He works as an information technology consultant in the United States, where there are limitless opportunities for well-trained experts in that field. He is married to Mary Nwanne, a former banker and accountant. They have two children.

Chiamaka also went down the IT route. In secondary school, she was an all-rounder, equally good in science and arts subjects. She not only found science challenging and interesting but was enticed by the promise and possibilities IT offered. She went for it and never looked back. She now works as a digital and change consultant across different organisations in the United Kingdom. Chiamaka is married to Ogemdi Okafor, an electrical engineer now working on strategic project delivery in the rail sector. They are blessed with three children.

Kenechukwu, true to his major in business administration, has an uncanny ability to adapt to any area of business. A well-trained marketing man, he has succeeded in achieving a seamless adaptation in the clinical trial of new drugs. Before approval by authorised departments, he collaborates with the drug makers and doctors. He also operates as a contractor in this area. He lives in the United States with his wife, Ihuoma, who works in the same field. They have other business interests and are blessed with four children.

The Knights of St John exemplify the theological virtues of the Roman Catholic faith. Florence and I became members, recommended by our priest and a knight of St John of good standing. We aim to put our Catholic faith into action. Our faith influences the way we lead our lives. Our hope sustains us – the hope that one day we will see the glory of God. We are devoted to acts of charity. Our patron saint is St John the Baptist, and through his intercession, we pray that our lives reflect the voice of one calling and preparing the way for the Lord. We strive to foster fraternity amongst the knights and to advance the spiritual and material interests of the church. It is important to us to improve the moral, mental and social conditions of our fellow knights. We all aim to support each other and our families, extending to the world the spirit of goodwill.

After strict interviews, we were initiated as knights of the church, to evangelise by our actions and words. We assist the various parishes in organising church events and assist in development where we can. There are five degrees – the fourth degree is the Order of the Chevalier and the fifth is the Noble Degree. The Jewel of Honour is awarded for outstanding service and devotion.

Through this organisation, I am known as Sir Dan, Jewel of Honour, Knight of St John's International, and my wife is Lady Florence. Currently, she is the grand respected president of the Knights of St John International, Abuja Grand Ladies Auxiliary.

Ify at her wedding

Chidubem at his wedding

Chiamaka at her wedding

Family portrait taken after Dube's wedding

Kene at his wedding

7

THE 19TH HOLE

I have been proud to sit on various boards throughout my career. A game of golf requires discipline of mind and planning, and I knew that I needed to gain as much experience as possible and to plan carefully in order to progress in my career.

I had developed so many skills during my educational years, and I wanted to use them to better myself and to better life for my family – yet I also wanted to help create a better world for everyone else. I wanted to go the extra mile, so in Zambia I was proud to represent INDECO on the boards of directors of several companies. The work was time-consuming but incredibly interesting and varied. The companies included Indeni Petroleum Refinery Ltd, Livingstone Motor Assemblies Ltd, which assembled Fiat cars, Chilanga Cement Manufacturing Company, Zamefa Electrical Cable Manufacturer and Mansa Battery Manufacturing Company.

Each time I sat on a board I learnt so much, and I

trust I helped others by sharing my continually increasing knowledge and company understanding. The debates I had so enjoyed earlier in life had assisted me in the ability to appreciate both sides of an argument, and I felt that I could bring non-biased opinions to the table. On my return to Nigeria, I was, at various times, on the boards of the following companies, among others: National Science and Technology Fund, Premier Breweries Company, Life Brewery Company, Niger Steel Company, Emenite, NACCIMA as well as being a council member of the Nigerian Stock Exchange. I always felt a strong duty of loyalty and care to all these companies. During my various employment experiences and from my university training, I had become an independent thinker and was able to have the courage of my convictions so that I could offer clear guidance. I could ask tough questions if necessary, and I was not impulsive in my decisions but would allow them due reflection.

I have also been a member of several organisations during my life because I have always wanted to share the benefits I have received by working with others; community spirit is extremely important to me. Therefore, I joined the Nigerian Society of Engineers, CKC Old Boys Association, Sports Club, Obosi Development Union. I was variously the tennis and golf captain of Enugu Sports Club. In 2011 I was honoured with admission into revered Eze na Ndi Ichie (Igwe-in-Council) of Obosi and capped by Igwe Chidubem Iweka 111 with the traditional title of Affaa Obosi as a result of my many contributions to the development of my town.

I have always tried to assimilate new concepts and developments with an intellectual curiosity. Just as in golf one is always looking to perfect their game, I have constantly strived, with a strong altruistic awareness, to improve in every area of life. Membership of boards and organisations was a crucial aspect of my professional career and provided many networking opportunities. Membership promoted the message that I was serious about my profession, and I appreciated the avenue to give back to my profession too.

Sir Dan and Lady Florence in their KSJI full uniform

In full Knights of St. John Int'l Uniform

Top: Putting on the golf course! Bottom: Teeing off!

A fight in a golf tournament. F
rom left: Dr Tim Menakaya, Arc Lot, Chief Paul Ibeku, Engr Dan Chuke

In traditional regalia, as Affaa-Obosi

With Senator Nnamdi Eriobuna

Flight at IBB Golf Club. From left:
Chief Tony Mba, Chief Ike Ndeokwelu, Engr. Williams, Engr. Dan Chuke

8

A GREAT ROUND

A great round of golf is not all about the score; it is about enjoying the company of others, appreciating the discipline of body and mind, enjoying a challenge, recognising the need to practice and learning to relax plus many more aspects, which will differ for each golfer. My life has been a great round so far, but I have plans for many more rounds of life yet! There was one occasion where I failed to complete my swing. I had obtained my nomination form to run for governor of Anambra State. The political terrain was rough as there were many desperate candidates who wanted it by any means. Because of the apparent risk to life, my family dissuaded me from going forward with it. Without the crystal glass to see the future or the ability to move back in time, I am not able to tell if my decision was right.

Florence and I keep busy with multiple engagements and events – life is hectic, but that is the way we like it. We have 15 amazing grandchildren spread across the globe, and it is awesome to imagine how many Chuke descendants will populate the earth several generations down the course, hopefully all following the standards that we have passed down in our family from generation to generation.

Our families have always been the most precious treasures to us, so it was a heartache when we lost our mother in 1991, aged 83, and Florence's mother in 1994. Our grief was still raw when we lost my father-in-law in 1996, my sister Agatha in 1998 and my brother Paul in 2000. All our ancestors live on in our memories and we take inspiration from the lives they led and show gratitude by regular reference to shared times with them. We are thankful for all they provided for us to ensure we had the best possible start in life. My siblings and I have always maintained a close contact, and I am happy to say that my 91 year old sister and my immediate elder brother at 82 are still enjoying life .

In addition to my family, I have been blessed with several incredibly supportive friends and colleagues. My managing director at INDECO in Zambia, Andrew Elias Kashita, was a mechanical engineer who had studied at Reading in the United Kingdom. He took a great fraternal interest in me and opened so many doors of opportunity for me. He gave me a lot of responsibility, placing in me his full trust as we travelled globally on business together, developing my confidence further as he introduced me to boardroom nuances. I can honestly say that Andrew played a huge part in me becoming the person I am today. Sadly, Andrew passed away in 2020, aged 87.

Peter Chigbo was the excellent boss who recruited me into Central Investment Company Limited on my return to Nigeria. He constantly provided me with opportunities to advance my career, boosting my confidence through his full support. I had only been employed by the company for three years when he recommended me to take over from him as CEO.

Austin Ugwumba was my close, older friend who thoroughly showed me the meaning of the phrase, 'Make new friends but keep the old – some are silver, the others gold!' Austin was truly a friend made of gold as he shared with me his wise words of counsel, which were invaluable to me on several important life occasions. I always relied on Austin for advice on professional issues and career guidance. He was always somebody I knew I could turn to if any personal issues should arise!

The pandemic has naturally been life-changing for us all. We were grateful for the vaccination programmes, and we ensure that we assist our health as much as possible through our diets and medications. I take vitamin C, zinc and various supplements to help to boost my immunity.

Before COVID-19, we visited the United Kingdom and the United States on a regular basis to spend time with our children and their families. Sadly, we have not done so since 2019. My intention is to travel again this year 2022 to see all my children. I usually stay 10–15 days with each offspring.

We are fortunate to have such beautiful locations to visit, including Florida, Texas and Virginia, in addition to London. Florence and I won't leave Nigeria to live elsewhere now because home is home. I'd like to travel again to sightsee and to visit Japan, Singapore, Malaysia and Vietnam – all places I have passed through on business but never really stayed to explore.

I help to resolve village disputes as a member of the cabinet. I still dream of seeing Nigeria become an industrial nation. I know we have not used all our nation's resources yet to the level I'd like to see them used. I'm happy to contribute in any way I can in the hope we can accomplish this and for Nigeria to continue to develop as it is such a beautiful and wondrous country, which offers so much potential. I respect that everyone's journey is different, and I believe we can find our own happiness within ourselves, but Florence and I acknowledge our full happiness comes from above.

I like to keep abreast of world news. I enjoy watching history documentaries, and I love listening to various debates. Reading novels is a pastime I enjoy. I follow the foreign markets and financial exchanges and enjoy dabbling in investments. Sport has played such a major role in my life. I loved playing tennis and would have continued to do so for longer if I had not suffered from back problems. I recall how, when diving to retrieve a drop shot from my opponent, a little sound emanated from my lower back. For a while I did not pay any attention to it, only to find that after the next two shots I could hardly move around the court. I sat down to rest in the club house hoping that the sensation of pain would soon go away. It didn't; instead, it kept increasing, so much that by the time I decided to go home, getting into my car was a crippling experience. I was told later that I had slipped disc or hernia of the vertebral disks. After my treatment at the orthopaedic hospital, it kept on repeating itself every time I either jumped up to serve the ball or tried to retrieve a drop shot so I was forced to stop playing tennis.

For a time, I was restless trying to find the sport I could engage in without the risk of exacerbating the back injury. About 200 metres down the road from my house in Enugu was the golf section of Enugu Sports Club and I decided to try it though I had not played the sport again since my days in New Zealand when I had a few hits at the range. I enrolled and soon the challenge became an obsession. So, golf is now my love and I play three times per week as a member of IBB International Golf and Country club in Abuja, named after the former president Ibrahim Badamosi Babangida. My best ever handicap was 14!

My faith has sustained me throughout my life. It has guided me, and as Martin Luther King pointed out, it involves taking the first step even when one can't see the whole staircase. Our involvement with the Knights of St John International is central to our lives.

In closing, I have thought about including a message for

my children and grandchildren, but actions speak stronger than words, and through the love and upbringing Florence and I have given them, they will find their own correct paths. Smiles are contagious, and our children have much to smile about. They have all discovered that kindness is free and that they can only fail if they quit; they all have strong work ethics. The positive thoughts with which we have raised them have created positive actions. We have every faith and confidence in all of them, knowing that, as we let go of their hands, they will plan their own shots well. As they tread the fairways of life, they are all quite capable of playing their own ball of choice and aiming for their own holes in one! We wish them all health, success, happiness, love and the gift of faith.

Story Terrace

Printed in Great Britain
by Amazon

10871201R00066